EMMANUEL JOSEPH

Blessed Business, Fostering Spiritual and Entrepreneurial Growth in Children

Copyright © 2025 by Emmanuel Joseph

All rights reserved. No part of this publication may be reproduced, stored or transmitted in any form or by any means, electronic, mechanical, photocopying, recording, scanning, or otherwise without written permission from the publisher. It is illegal to copy this book, post it to a website, or distribute it by any other means without permission.

First edition

This book was professionally typeset on Reedsy.
Find out more at reedsy.com

Contents

1. Chapter 1 — 1
2. Chapter 1: The Seeds of Faith and Fortune — 3
3. Chapter 2: The Power of Prayer and Perseverance — 5
4. Chapter 3: The Entrepreneurial Spirit in Daily Life — 7
5. Chapter 4: Trust and Teamwork — 9
6. Chapter 5: Moral Integrity and Business Ethics — 11
7. Chapter 6: Education as a Lifelong Journey — 13
8. Chapter 7: Compassion in Commerce — 15
9. Chapter 8: Family Values and Business Balance — 17
10. Chapter 9: Overcoming Fear and Taking Risks — 19
11. Chapter 10: Mentorship and Guiding the Next Generation — 21
12. Chapter 11: Embracing Change and Innovation — 22
13. Chapter 12: Spiritual Reflections in Business Decisions — 23
14. Chapter 13: Celebrating Success and Giving Thanks — 24
15. Chapter 14: Leaving a Legacy of Love and Wisdom — 25
16. Chapter 15: The Endless Journey of Growth — 26

1

Chapter 1

Introduction

In the heart of a small, peaceful village by the river, a young boy named Akin embarked on a remarkable journey that would transform his life and the lives of many around him. Raised by a humble farmer, Akin's childhood was filled with lessons of hard work, faith, and the beauty of nature. His father's words of wisdom, spoken amidst the rustling leaves and the rhythm of their labor, planted the seeds of spiritual growth and entrepreneurial spirit within him.

From an early age, Akin learned that faith was like planting seeds in fertile soil. It required patience, dedication, and a hopeful heart, just as nurturing crops did. This profound understanding of faith as an integral part of daily life became the foundation upon which Akin would build his future endeavors. As he grew older, the lessons of his father remained etched in his heart, guiding him through life's challenges and opportunities.

Akin's village, while picturesque, faced its share of hardships. The villagers, with their untapped talents and resources, often struggled to make ends meet. Observing their resilience and potential, Akin was inspired to help them harness their skills and create prosperous, fulfilling lives. He envisioned a community where spiritual growth and entrepreneurial success went hand in hand, each nurturing and supporting the other.

As Akin ventured into the world of entrepreneurship, he discovered that true success was not measured by wealth alone but by the positive impact one could have on others. He began organizing workshops and sharing stories of successful entrepreneurs, igniting a spark of possibility within the villagers. His approach was holistic, blending practical skills with spiritual insights, and fostering a culture of collaboration and mutual support.

Akin's journey was not without its challenges. Natural disasters, ethical dilemmas, and the ever-present fear of failure tested his resolve. However, his unwavering faith and perseverance carried him through these trials. He turned to prayer for strength and guidance, finding solace in the connection to a higher power. Akin's story of resilience and determination became a beacon of hope for the village, inspiring others to face their own challenges with courage and conviction.

Through his efforts, Akin transformed his village into a thriving community of innovators and compassionate individuals. The cooperative bakery, the community library, the eco-friendly farming initiative—each venture was a testament to the power of faith, integrity, and teamwork. Akin's emphasis on trust, compassion, and continuous learning created a ripple effect, touching the lives of children and adults alike.

As Akin grew older, he reflected on his journey and the legacy he wanted to leave. Documenting his experiences, lessons, and values in a book, he hoped to inspire future generations to pursue their dreams while staying true to their spiritual and ethical foundations. "Blessed Business: Fostering Spiritual and Entrepreneurial Growth in Children" is a celebration of Akin's life and the profound impact one individual can have on a community. It serves as a guiding light for all who seek to blend faith and entrepreneurship, creating a brighter future for themselves and those around them.

2

Chapter 1: The Seeds of Faith and Fortune

In a small village nestled by the river, there lived a boy named Akin. His father, a humble farmer, would often take him to the fields and teach him the value of hard work. The father-son duo spent many mornings together, planting seeds and tending to the crops. One day, as they were working under the warm sun, his father shared a valuable lesson. He explained that nurturing the crops was much like nurturing one's faith—both required patience, dedication, and hope for a fruitful harvest.

Akin was mesmerized by his father's words and began to understand the deeper connection between their daily tasks and spiritual growth. He realized that just as the seeds needed water and care to grow, his spirit needed faith and love to flourish. This lesson stayed with Akin, guiding him as he grew into a thoughtful and enterprising young man.

As Akin matured, he noticed that the villagers often faced challenges and hardships. Inspired by his father's teachings, he decided to help his community find ways to improve their lives. He started small, offering to help neighbors with their gardens and sharing the knowledge he had gained from his father. Through these simple acts of kindness, Akin began to see the potential for positive change.

One day, Akin came across a group of children playing by the river. They were full of energy and curiosity, but many lacked direction and purpose. Akin saw an opportunity to teach them the same values his father had instilled in him. He gathered the children and shared stories of faith, hard work, and perseverance. He encouraged them to dream big and believe in their potential.

The children were captivated by Akin's stories and eager to learn more. They began to see the world through a new lens, understanding that their actions could have a significant impact on their lives and their community. Akin continued to mentor the children, providing guidance and support as they explored their interests and talents.

Through these efforts, Akin realized that fostering spiritual and entrepreneurial growth in children was a powerful way to create lasting change. By nurturing their faith and encouraging them to pursue their dreams, he was planting the seeds for a brighter future. As the children grew, so did their aspirations, and the village began to thrive.

The lessons Akin learned in the fields with his father had come full circle. The seeds of faith and fortune he had planted in the hearts of the children were beginning to bear fruit, and the village was reaping the rewards of their collective efforts.

3

Chapter 2: The Power of Prayer and Perseverance

Young Akin faced many challenges throughout his journey. One year, a powerful storm swept through the village, devastating his family's crops and leaving them with little to sustain themselves. Despite the hardships, Akin turned to prayer, seeking strength and guidance from a higher power. He realized that prayer was more than just asking for help; it was a way to connect with the divine and find inner resilience.

Inspired by his newfound strength, Akin helped his father rebuild their farm. They worked tirelessly, replanting crops and repairing damage. Akin's perseverance and faith proved to be a source of motivation for his family and the village. They began to see that with spiritual strength and unwavering determination, any adversity could be overcome.

Akin's story of resilience spread throughout the village, inspiring others to face their own challenges with hope and perseverance. It became clear that the power of prayer and hard work could lead to remarkable transformations, both in the fields and in the hearts of the villagers.

One such transformation occurred when a young girl named Amara, who had lost her parents, found solace in Akin's guidance. Akin took her under his wing, teaching her the importance of faith and perseverance. With his support, Amara began to excel in her studies and discovered her talent for painting.

Her artwork became a source of inspiration for the village, demonstrating the profound impact of prayer and perseverance.

Through these stories and experiences, Akin showed that spiritual growth and entrepreneurial success were deeply intertwined. By nurturing both aspects, individuals could overcome any obstacle and create a better future for themselves and their community.

4

Chapter 3: The Entrepreneurial Spirit in Daily Life

As Akin grew older, he noticed that many villagers had untapped talents and resources. He saw an opportunity to help them create small businesses that could thrive. Akin believed that entrepreneurship was not just about making money but about serving the community and uplifting others.

He began organizing workshops, where he taught practical skills and shared stories of successful entrepreneurs. One such story was about a woman named Mariam, who turned her love for baking into a profitable business. With Akin's guidance, Mariam's bakery flourished, providing her family with a stable income and bringing joy to the villagers with her delicious treats.

Through these efforts, Akin inspired many to see the potential within themselves and their surroundings. The village gradually transformed into a hub of creativity and innovation, with each new business contributing to the community's growth and prosperity. Children and adults alike began to explore their interests and develop their skills, finding new ways to support themselves and their families.

Akin's approach to entrepreneurship was holistic, emphasizing the importance of personal growth and community well-being. He taught that true success was measured not only by financial gain but by the positive impact one could have on others. By nurturing the entrepreneurial spirit in daily life, Akin helped create a culture of collaboration and mutual support.

One memorable initiative was a craft fair, where villagers showcased their handmade goods. The event was a resounding success, fostering a sense of pride and accomplishment among the participants. Akin's leadership and encouragement had empowered the villagers to believe in their abilities and strive for excellence.

5

Chapter 4: Trust and Teamwork

Akin's next venture was a cooperative bakery, bringing together talented bakers from the village. He emphasized the importance of trust and teamwork, likening it to a spiritual journey where every member had a unique role. Akin led by example, fostering a sense of unity and shared purpose.

One of the bakers, Sani, was initially skeptical about working in a team. He preferred to work alone, fearing that others might not share his dedication to quality. However, Akin encouraged Sani to trust his colleagues and see the potential benefits of collaboration.

Over time, Sani began to appreciate the strengths of his fellow bakers. He realized that working together allowed them to produce better products and serve more customers. The bakery flourished, not only because of the delicious bread but also because of the harmonious collaboration that infused every loaf with love and dedication.

Akin's emphasis on trust and teamwork extended beyond the bakery. He organized community activities that brought people together, fostering a sense of belonging and shared responsibility. By building strong relationships and working together, the villagers achieved more than they ever could individually.

The success of the cooperative bakery became a model for other ventures in the village. People began to see the value of collaboration and mutual support, applying these principles to their own businesses and daily lives. Akin's vision of a united and thriving community was becoming a reality.

6

Chapter 5: Moral Integrity and Business Ethics

One day, a wealthy merchant visited the village and offered to buy the bakery, promising Akin immense wealth. However, the merchant's practices were known to be unethical, and Akin faced a moral dilemma. Remembering the teachings of his father and the power of prayer, he chose to uphold his principles and rejected the offer.

This decision reinforced the value of integrity and ethics in business, showing that true success is measured by the impact on others and staying true to one's beliefs. Akin's choice inspired the villagers to prioritize ethical practices in their own ventures, creating a community built on trust and respect.

Akin's commitment to moral integrity was tested again when a rival bakery opened in the village. The new bakery used questionable tactics to attract customers, but Akin remained steadfast in his principles. He focused on providing quality products and excellent service, trusting that his customers would appreciate the difference.

In time, the rival bakery's unethical practices were exposed, and Akin's bakery emerged stronger than ever. The villagers recognized the value of integrity and chose to support businesses that upheld their values. Akin's example demonstrated that ethical business practices could lead to long-term success and respect within the community.

Through these experiences, Akin taught the importance of moral integrity and business ethics. He showed that staying true to one's beliefs and prioritizing the well-being of others could lead to a prosperous and fulfilling life. His unwavering commitment to his principles became a guiding light for the village, inspiring others to follow his example.

7

Chapter 6: Education as a Lifelong Journey

Realizing the importance of continuous learning, Akin started a community library. He encouraged children to explore books on various subjects, blending spiritual and entrepreneurial knowledge. Akin believed that education was a lifelong journey that empowered individuals to make informed decisions and innovate.

The library became a hub of knowledge, inspiring young minds to dream big and pursue their passions with a strong moral compass. One young girl, Fatima, discovered her love for science and began conducting experiments in the library's small lab. With Akin's encouragement, Fatima's curiosity grew, and she eventually earned a scholarship to study at a renowned university.

Through the library, Akin helped children realize that their dreams were within reach. He taught them that with faith, dedication, and continuous learning, they could achieve remarkable things and make a positive impact on the world.

Akin's vision for the library extended beyond books. He organized workshops and seminars, inviting experts from various fields to share their knowledge and experiences. These events provided valuable opportunities for the villagers to learn new skills and stay updated on the latest developments in their areas of interest.

The library also became a place for spiritual growth and reflection. Akin arranged for spiritual leaders to hold discussions and meditation sessions, fostering a sense of inner peace and balance. By integrating spiritual and entrepreneurial education, Akin created a holistic environment that nurtured the mind, body, and soul.

8

Chapter 7: Compassion in Commerce

Akin's compassion extended beyond his ventures. He often organized charity events, using the bakery's profits to support the less fortunate. He taught that true wealth was found in the joy of giving and uplifting others.

One memorable event was a fundraiser for a neighboring village affected by a severe drought. Akin and the villagers rallied together, baking bread and organizing a market to raise funds. The event was a resounding success, providing much-needed relief to the drought-stricken village and strengthening the bonds between the communities.

Akin's approach to commerce, rooted in compassion, showed that businesses could thrive while making a positive impact on society. His story spread, inspiring neighboring villages to adopt similar practices and create a network of support and generosity.

Akin's compassion was also evident in his daily interactions. He made it a point to know his customers personally, understanding their needs and finding ways to help them. Whether it was offering a free loaf of bread to a struggling family or providing employment opportunities to those in need, Akin's actions spoke volumes about his commitment to uplifting others.

Through his compassionate approach to commerce, Akin demonstrated that business success and social responsibility could go hand in hand. He taught that by caring for others and contributing to the greater good, one could create a lasting legacy of love and kindness.

9

Chapter 8: Family Values and Business Balance

Akin balanced his entrepreneurial pursuits with his family life, cherishing moments with his loved ones. He taught his children the same values he learned from his father, blending faith and entrepreneurial spirit. Family gatherings became opportunities to share stories, discuss ideas, and strengthen their bonds.

One evening, around the dinner table, Akin's daughter, Zainab, shared her dream of starting a pottery business. Akin encouraged her, offering guidance and support as she pursued her passion. Together, they turned a small corner of their home into a pottery studio, where Zainab's creativity flourished.

Akin's children grew up appreciating the harmony between personal values and professional endeavors, carrying on his legacy. They learned that true success was found in the balance between family, faith, and entrepreneurship.

Akin's commitment to his family extended beyond his immediate household. He maintained close relationships with his extended family, ensuring that everyone felt supported and included. Family reunions were filled with laughter, storytelling, and the sharing of wisdom across generations.

Through these gatherings, Akin emphasized the importance of maintaining strong family ties and supporting one another. He taught that a close-knit family provided a foundation of love and stability, enabling individuals to pursue their dreams with confidence.

10

Chapter 9: Overcoming Fear and Taking Risks

One of Akin's boldest ventures was establishing an eco-friendly farming initiative. Despite initial fears and doubts, he trusted in his vision and the power of prayer. Akin took calculated risks, learning from failures and celebrating successes.

The initiative faced many challenges, from skeptical villagers to unpredictable weather. However, Akin's determination and faith kept him going. He experimented with new farming techniques, eventually creating a sustainable model that benefited both the environment and the community.

Akin's journey showed that overcoming fear and taking risks was essential for growth, both spiritually and entrepreneurially. His success inspired others to pursue their own ambitious projects, knowing that with faith and perseverance, they too could achieve great things.

One of the key components of the eco-friendly farming initiative was the introduction of organic farming practices. Akin organized workshops to educate farmers on the benefits of organic methods, reducing the use of harmful chemicals and improving soil health. The transition was challenging, but Akin's unwavering support and encouragement motivated the farmers to persevere.

The success of the eco-friendly farming initiative had a ripple effect on the village. It not only improved the quality of the produce but also attracted attention from neighboring communities and organizations. Akin's willingness to take risks and embrace new techniques paid off, resulting in higher yields and healthier crops. This success encouraged other villages to adopt similar practices, leading to a wider movement towards sustainable agriculture. Akin's story demonstrated that overcoming fear and taking risks could lead to significant advancements and positive change.

Akin's initiative also included a mentoring program for young farmers. He paired experienced farmers with novices, fostering a sense of community and shared learning. This mentorship program not only improved farming practices but also strengthened the bonds between villagers, creating a supportive environment where everyone thrived.

11

Chapter 10: Mentorship and Guiding the Next Generation

As Akin's reputation grew, he became a mentor to many young entrepreneurs, sharing his wisdom and experiences. He believed in guiding the next generation with patience and understanding, fostering their growth.

One of his mentees, Musa, was a young man with a passion for technology. Akin encouraged Musa to explore his interests and provided him with resources to develop his skills. With Akin's guidance, Musa created a successful tech startup that brought innovative solutions to the village.

Akin's mentorship extended beyond business, helping young individuals navigate life's challenges with faith and resilience. His impact was profound, creating a ripple effect of positive change that continued to inspire future generations.

Akin also established a mentorship network, connecting aspiring entrepreneurs with experienced mentors from various fields. This network provided valuable guidance and support, helping young entrepreneurs overcome obstacles and achieve their goals. Akin's dedication to mentorship ensured that the village's legacy of innovation and success would continue for generations to come.

12

Chapter 11: Embracing Change and Innovation

As times changed, Akin embraced new technologies and innovative ideas. He encouraged the village to adapt and evolve, blending traditional practices with modern advancements.

Akin's openness to change ensured that the community remained vibrant and competitive. He introduced solar energy solutions, improving the quality of life for the villagers and reducing their dependence on non-renewable resources.

His story highlighted the importance of flexibility and innovation in sustaining growth and prosperity. Akin's ability to adapt and innovate kept the village thriving, setting an example for others to follow.

Akin also promoted the use of digital tools and platforms to enhance business operations. He organized training sessions to teach villagers how to leverage technology for marketing, communication, and financial management. By embracing change and innovation, Akin ensured that the village remained resilient and forward-thinking.

13

Chapter 12: Spiritual Reflections in Business Decisions

Akin often took time for spiritual reflection, seeking clarity and guidance in his business decisions. He taught that spirituality was not separate from entrepreneurship but intertwined.

Through meditation and prayer, Akin found balance and purpose, making decisions that aligned with his values. One such decision was partnering with a fair-trade organization to ensure that the village's products reached a wider market while maintaining ethical practices.

Akin's approach showed that inner peace and spiritual grounding could lead to wise and impactful choices. His decisions were a testament to the power of integrating faith and entrepreneurship.

Akin also encouraged others to incorporate spiritual reflections into their daily routines. He organized meditation sessions and spiritual discussions, providing a space for individuals to connect with their inner selves and find guidance in their entrepreneurial endeavors. This holistic approach created a sense of harmony and purpose within the community.

14

Chapter 13: Celebrating Success and Giving Thanks

Akin celebrated successes with gratitude, recognizing the contributions of everyone involved. He organized community gatherings to acknowledge achievements and give thanks.

One such celebration was the anniversary of the cooperative bakery. The villagers came together to share stories, enjoy delicious food, and express their appreciation for one another. Akin's gratitude extended to small victories and everyday blessings, fostering a culture of appreciation and positivity.

His celebrations were reminders that success was a collective effort, rooted in gratitude. Akin's ability to celebrate and give thanks strengthened the bonds within the community and inspired others to adopt a similar mindset.

Akin's celebrations also included giving back to the community. He organized volunteer days, where villagers worked together on community projects, such as building a playground or cleaning up the riverbank. These activities not only improved the village but also fostered a sense of pride and unity among the residents.

15

Chapter 14: Leaving a Legacy of Love and Wisdom

As Akin grew older, he reflected on his journey and the legacy he wanted to leave. He documented his experiences, lessons, and values in a book, hoping to inspire future generations.

Akin's legacy was one of love, wisdom, and a harmonious blend of spiritual and entrepreneurial growth. His story became a guiding light for many, illuminating the path to a meaningful and fulfilling life.

One of his most cherished memories was passing on his book to his grandchildren. They listened intently as he shared stories of his journey, absorbing the valuable lessons he had learned along the way. Akin's grandchildren were inspired to carry on his legacy, embodying the principles of faith, compassion, and entrepreneurship.

Akin's impact extended beyond his family, reaching the wider community and beyond. His book became a source of inspiration for many, guiding them on their own journeys of growth and fulfillment.

16

Chapter 15: The Endless Journey of Growth

Akin's story is a testament to the endless journey of growth—both spiritual and entrepreneurial. His life shows that with faith, perseverance, compassion, and integrity, one can create a lasting impact. Akin's journey continues to inspire, reminding us that fostering spiritual and entrepreneurial growth in children is a blessed endeavor that shapes the future.

The village, once a quiet and humble place, had transformed into a thriving community of innovators and compassionate individuals. Akin's teachings had taken root, guiding the villagers to pursue their dreams while remaining grounded in their values.

Akin's legacy lived on through the countless lives he had touched. His story serves as a reminder that the seeds of faith and fortune, when nurtured with love and dedication, can grow into a powerful force for good. The journey of growth, both spiritual and entrepreneurial, is indeed a blessed one that can shape a brighter future for all.

Book Description

Blessed Business: Fostering Spiritual and Entrepreneurial Growth in Children is an inspiring and heartfelt journey into the life of Akin, a boy from a small village who learns the profound connection between faith

CHAPTER 15: THE ENDLESS JOURNEY OF GROWTH

and entrepreneurship. Guided by the wisdom of his humble farmer father, Akin's story unfolds with lessons of patience, dedication, and hope—essential elements for nurturing both the spirit and one's dreams.

This engaging book follows Akin's transformation from a curious child into a thoughtful and enterprising young man. Along the way, Akin faces numerous challenges, from natural disasters that threaten his family's livelihood to ethical dilemmas that test his integrity. Through it all, Akin relies on the power of prayer, perseverance, and the unwavering support of his community.

Akin's journey is not just about personal success; it's about uplifting others and creating a thriving, compassionate community. As he organizes workshops, starts cooperative ventures, and mentors young entrepreneurs, Akin's influence spreads, igniting a spirit of innovation and collaboration among the villagers. Each chapter weaves together touching stories and practical advice, showcasing how spiritual growth and entrepreneurial endeavors can go hand in hand.

Throughout the book, readers will discover the importance of trust, teamwork, continuous learning, and moral integrity. Akin's compassionate approach to commerce and his dedication to family values provide a holistic perspective on achieving true success. His legacy of love, wisdom, and a harmonious blend of spirituality and entrepreneurship serves as a guiding light for future generations.

"Blessed Business: Fostering Spiritual and Entrepreneurial Growth in Children" is a celebration of the endless journey of growth, both spiritual and entrepreneurial. It's a testament to the power of faith, perseverance, compassion, and integrity in shaping a brighter future for individuals and communities alike. Whether you're a parent, educator, or aspiring entrepreneur, Akin's story will inspire and guide you on your own path to meaningful and fulfilling success.

www.ingramcontent.com/pod-product-compliance
Lightning Source LLC
LaVergne TN
LVHW020741090526
838202LV00057BA/6168